GERMS
The Library of Disease-Causing Organisms™

THE WAR AGAINST GERMS

Josepha Sherman

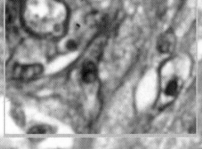

Published in 2004 by The Rosen Publishing Group, Inc.
29 East 21st Street, New York, NY 10010

First Edition

Library of Congress Cataloging-in-Publication Data

Sherman, Josepha.
The war against germs/Josepha Sherman.—1st ed.
    p. cm.—(Germs: The library of disease-causing organisms)
Includes bibliographical references and index.
Contents: What are germs?—Germ fighting in ancient and medieval history—Germ fighting in modern history—The future of germ fighting.
ISBN 0-8239-4495-6 (library binding)
1. Medical microbiology—Juvenile literature. 2. Communicable diseases—Juvenile literature. 3. Antibiotics—Juvenile literature. 4. Immunity—Juvenile literature. [1. Communicable diseases. 2. Diseases. 3. Bacteria. 4. Microorganisms. 5. Antibiotics. 6. Immunity.]
I. Title. II. Series.
QR46.S525 2004
616'.01—dc21
                                                                2003009379

Manufactured in the United States of America

On the cover: A scanning electron microscope photograph of the smallpox virus

CONTENTS

1 *What Are Germs?*

We use the word "germ" to mean many things. We say we have the germ of an idea, meaning we've come up with the beginning of an idea. But when someone says, "I caught a germ," we instantly know that this means sickness. Germ is the blanket name we use when we refer to bacteria, fungi, microbes, protozoa, viruses, and other disease-causing microorganisms. What all these different types of germs have in common is that they are all very tiny.

Germs are single-celled organisms, living things that are made up of only one cell apiece. They are too small to be seen by the naked eye, though they can be seen through a microscope. This is why they are also called microbes. Germs are amazing things, truly a look into the past, since they are probably the oldest forms of life on Earth. In fact, some families of germs may have been around for billions of years—far longer than most animals or any humans. They are also probably the most numerous living things on the planet. Today, there are billions of germs in everything, from water to soil to air, as well as in and on every living thing. So far, more than

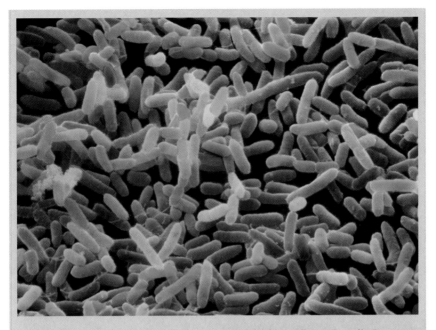

An electron micrograph of the bacteria *Escherichia coli*, or *E. coli*. In 1885, German bacteriologist Theodor Escherich discovered that some strains of *E. coli* were responsible for infant diarrhea and gastroenteritis. Most *E. coli* strains are harmless or even beneficial. The dangerous strains are mutations and can be transmitted through contaminated food or contact with infected people or the surfaces they have touched.

4,000 species of just bacteria have been identified, and that is probably not the total count.

This overwhelming number of germs isn't as frightening a fact as it sounds. Fortunately for other living creatures on Earth, more than 95 percent of germs are harmless. Some germs are even "good germs" necessary for animal life. One type of germ, for instance, helps with the digestion of food. Other types cause the decay of dead plants and animals back into the soil, and by doing so help make the soil fertile. Still other types of germs curdle milk into cheese or yogurt. Specialized germs live in the human mouth and fight off disease-causing germs, and even more specialized organisms live at the roots of human eyelashes and keep the lashes clean and healthy.

But there are germs that are dangerous—even fatal—to living creatures. Dangerous bacteria can cause diseases and problems such as strep throat, pneumonia, diphtheria, and tetanus. They can also quickly multiply in improperly cleaned or stored food and cause the unpleasant and sometimes deadly problem called food poisoning. Dangerous viruses can cause diseases as mild as the common cold and as serious as influenza—the flu. They can also cause chicken pox, measles, mumps, and the incurable disease AIDS, which is caused by the human immunodeficiency virus (HIV). Scientists even suspect that some viruses may cause some types of cancer. Protozoa can spread disease through contaminated water. Some protozoa cause intestinal infections leading to pain and diarrhea.

An electron micrograph of the rubella virus, which causes German measles. If a woman contracts German measles while pregnant, her baby may be born handicapped or brain damaged.

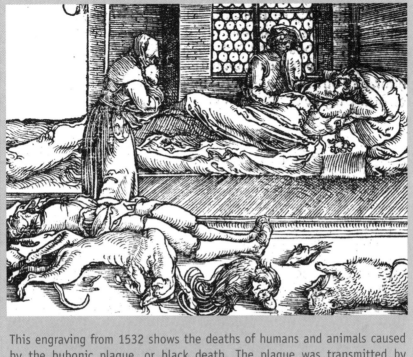

This engraving from 1532 shows the deaths of humans and animals caused by the bubonic plague, or black death. The plague was transmitted by infected fleas carrying the *Yersinia pestis* bacteria. Occasional plague outbreaks still occur, but they are rare and usually happen in rural areas. If caught in time, plague can be successfully treated with antibiotics.

Over the centuries, dangerous germs have killed hundreds of thousands of people. More people died in the Spanish flu epidemic of 1914, which took place during World War I, than were killed in battle in the war. The black death (bubonic plague), which happened in the fourteenth century, was caused by contagious—that is, easily spread—bacteria, and killed one-fourth of the population of Europe. Today, people die from AIDS, the flu, and many other diseases that are caused by dangerous germs.

Our bodies have a natural defense system against harmful germs. This is called the immune system. It is a complicated and amazing network of cells and organs that work together. The immune system guards the body against attacks by "foreign" invaders—and this means that the immune system has to have a sense of what is "self" and what isn't. This doesn't mean that every cell is actually able to think, "I'm me!" Instead, each cell contains specific molecules, tiny bits of matter that identify it as belonging to the body. The immune system normally doesn't attack any cells that have the right identification. Because the immune system doesn't attack those other body cells, it is said that the immune cells and the other body cells keep in a balance known as self-tolerance.

Amazingly enough, the immune system can and will react to millions of "non-self" germs and fights them off by creating special substances and cells called antibodies. When the system works, these antibodies catch and destroy all the outside germs. While this response is nothing short of wonderful when it comes to fighting off dangerous germs, it can be a problem in the case of an organ transplant. When the immune system identifies the cells of a transplanted organ as invaders and tries to fight them off, the organ is said to be rejected by the body.

The body has immune organs all through it. These are called lymphoid organs, since they create and send out the lymphocytes. These are white blood cells, the "warriors" of the immune system. There are several types of white blood cells. The immune system response begins when a type of white blood cell called a macrophage encounters an invading germ and engulfs it. The macrophage then displays pieces of the "digested" germ on its surface. These pieces of the "dead" virus have now become an antigen. An antigen is anything that triggers the immune system to get to work.

Another type of white blood cell, the helper T cell, identifies the antigen, and the helper T cell joins the macrophage. As they unite, they produce chemicals that allow the white blood cells to "communicate." This communication causes more T cells to be created, both helper T cells and a different type, killer T cells. As they multiply, the helper T cells also give off chemicals that signal another type of white blood cell, the B cell, to multiply and produce antibodies. Antibodies are substances that fight germs. The B cells release their antibodies, which bind to the germs. The killer T cells punch holes in the

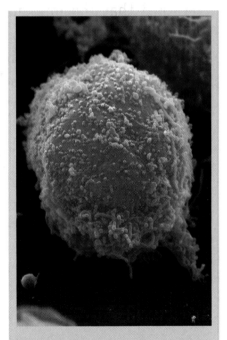

This white blood cell is infected with HIV. By killing or impairing T4 cells, the virus prevents the body from fighting off infections and cancers.

germs and any infected cells. Together, these cells kill off the invaders.

Once the invasion is over, another type of white blood cell, the suppressor T cell, "turns off" the T and B cells. But the system holds on to some "memory cells" so that it can respond more quickly if there's another attack.

There are some basic precautions that people can take to ward off germs. Simply washing hands thoroughly with soap and warm water cuts down the chance of illness. Thoroughly washing kitchen counters, cutting boards, and knives after cutting up raw meat also helps to remove germs that may be on raw food. Keeping food refrigerated or frozen keeps it safe until cooking. Food that's cooked at the right temperature and for the right length of time can't hold any germ surprises. The polite rule of covering your mouth when you sneeze or cough is one of the easiest ways to keep from spreading germs. Using a tissue, and then throwing it away, is good, too. Insect repellent and long sleeves help ward off disease-bearing mosquitoes and ticks.

But even with all this care, many germs are too dangerous for any simple means of protection to work. From the earliest days of history, humans knew that fighting disease—and germs in particular— would need to be a true war.

Germ Fighting in Ancient and Medieval History

Before the invention of the microscope at the end of the sixteenth century, doctors had no way of knowing about the existence of germs. They had no way to see something that tiny. This didn't mean that they weren't aware that something was causing disease and infection. In some parts of the ancient world, doctors worked around the lack of specific knowledge to come up with useful cures.

Ancient Mesopotamia

In ancient Mesopotamia, an area that includes most of the countries now in the Middle East, between 3000 and 1000 BC, disease was often thought to be caused by gods, demons, or spirits. However, doctors thought that specific gods or demons were responsible for specific diseases. In other words, supernatural figures were taking the place of germs in their belief system. But whatever they thought the cause, doctors worked to find ways to heal diseases and prevent infection. Much of the information about the medicines that they used has been lost, and

Before the invention of the microscope or modern medicines, healers in ancient times had to rely on guesswork, trial and error, and religious rituals. Still, Mesopotamian doctors and other early physicians discovered useful natural medicines, such as sesame oil, which has antibacterial properties.

identifying the different drugs is difficult, since there are no translations for the terms the doctors used.

We do know that there were two kinds of medical professionals. The first was the *ashipu*, who was responsible for finding out what supernatural force had caused the illness and whether the patient had committed any sins. The ashipu was also responsible for any spells or other magic thought necessary. The second medical practitioner was closer to what we think of as a doctor. This was the *asu*. Not only did the asu prescribe medicine, he also knew about the need to keep a wound clean, to wash everything, and to apply clean bandages.

An asu also knew how to make a healing plaster out of ingredients that would help fight off infection, and which herbs—such as garlic—had antibiotic or antiseptic uses.

Ancient Egypt

Like their counterparts in Mesopotamia, doctors in ancient Egypt didn't know about germs either. They didn't know what caused infections—they suspected evil supernatural forces were to blame—but that didn't stop them from understanding how to stop those infections. We know something about their practices from two doctors' manuals, called by the modern names of the Edwin Smith Papyrus and the Ebers Papyrus.

There were several classes of doctors. What we might call a general practitioner was called a *swnw*, or *sunu*. A doctor who specialized in magic as well as medicine was a *sau*. It was believed that medicine and magic went hand in hand. There were also as many medical specialists in ancient Egypt as there are nowadays, from surgeons to dentists.

When it came to fighting germs (even if they didn't know the concept), Egyptian doctors used antibiotic herbs such as garlic and antiseptics such as oil of fir, which was imported from Palestine. They knew that cleanliness kept away sickness, though not why. One of the most important remedies used to keep wounds free from infection and even scarring was honey. This wasn't modern honey from a jar, which can sometimes contain dangerous botulism spores, but pure honey. Today, doctors are starting to study the antibiotic properties of honey, which may even be strong enough to kill the toughest of germs.

Ancient Greece

While the Greeks admitted that the Egyptians were the finest doctors, the Greek doctor Hippocrates (c. 460 BC–c. 377 BC), who worked on the island of Cos, is often called the father of medicine, mostly because of the more than sixty medical books written by his followers. Hippocrates was the first to state that disease had nothing to do with gods or evil spirits, and to turn medicine into a science. However, he made a major mistake, coming up with the theory that the human body had four "humors," black bile, yellow bile,

Hippocrates was the first physician to accurately describe the symptoms of pneumonia and childhood epilepsy. He was also one of the first to believe that thoughts and emotions came from the brain and not the heart.

phlegm, and blood, and stating that illness occurred when one of these humors was out of balance. Hippocrates did stress the importance of fresh air, a good diet, and plenty of exercise to help the body heal itself.

The Middle Ages

During the Middle Ages, most of the advances in understanding how to fight infection and disease came from the Arab and Persian world.

Rhazes (al-Razi), who was born in AD 865 and died sometime around AD 925, was a Persian doctor who worked in the hospitals of Baghdad around AD 900. Not only did Rhazes translate some of the works of the Greek doctors, such as the followers of Hippocrates, he observed his patients carefully and took precise notes. He published his

The First Doctors

Hippocrates' students had to swear an oath to help their patients and do no harm before they could become doctors. Doctors today still swear a modern version of the Hippocratic oath.

In ancient Rome, Marcus Terentius Varro, who was born in 116 BC and died about 27 BC, was a scholar and accomplished writer known as the "most learned of the Romans." He came up with a concept that seems close to modern germ theory. Varro wrote that tiny creatures too small to be seen by the human eye lived in swampy areas, entered the human body through the mouth and nose, and caused disease. Another first-century AD writer, Lucius Junius Moderatus Columella, also theorized that disease might come in some way from marsh insects, or possibly other small creatures. But nothing really developed from these theories.

case studies, particularly the ones in which his careful observations led him to discover the difference between measles and smallpox. This marks one of the first written examples of a doctor identifying a specific disease. Rhaze's manual, *The Al-Hawi*, was widely read throughout medieval Europe, and his text on smallpox and measles was still in use in the eighteenth century.

Another famous Persian doctor was Avicenna (Ibn Sina), who was born in AD 980 and died in 1037. Avicenna wrote more than 200 books. The most famous was the *Canon*, a medical textbook that included both past information and new discoveries. It included such subjects as diseases, fevers, and remedies. Avicenna made a special point of the need for cleanliness during surgery to keep open wounds from becoming infected.

As a physician and scientist, Rhazes was far ahead of his time. Among other accomplishments, he was the first to recognize that fever was part of the body's defense mechanisms.

Meanwhile, in western Europe, many medieval doctors followed Hippocrates' idea of four humors within the human body. They also believed that disease was often caused not by outside sources, but by the sins of those who became sick. Because few people understood that cleanliness reduced disease, plagues could spread easily, especially through crowded cities like London. A nasty side effect of this problem included anti-Semitism. Bubonic plague, one of the great scourges of the Middle Ages, was spread by fleas and the rats that harbored the fleas. Since Jewish homes were kept free of rats and fleas, fewer Jews fell sick. The Jews, therefore, were blamed for the plague—just because they kept clean homes.

The Renaissance

In Italy during the Renaissance, Girolamo Fracastoro (1478–1553) was a multitalented man, a doctor, astronomer, philosopher, and poet. He theorized that infection was due to "seeds of disease," which were able to multiply within the body and pass on the disease through human breathing. But there was no way to prove his theories. Athanasius Kircher (1601–1680) was another multitalented man, a German writer and scientist who wrote a treatise on the bubonic plague of 1656. In it, he stated that tiny animals might have caused the plague.

But perhaps the most important figure of the era was Antonie van Leeuwenhoek of Holland (1632–1723).

Microscopes were actually invented more than forty years before Leeuwenhoek was born, but the lenses he ground were clearer and more powerful than anyone else's, allowing him to see more detail at greater magnification. He also hired illustrators to draw what could be seen through his microscopes, producing amazingly accurate images of microorganisms.

He was born into a merchant family and had no higher education. He never earned a degree from any university. But Leeuwenhoek was both intelligent and highly curious about the world around him. Even as he was making a living as a fabric merchant, he began learning how to grind glass lenses and then to make simple microscopes. He designed and built more than 500 microscopes during his life, and because of his skill in grinding lenses, he was able to make some that magnified more than 200 times. As a result, it was Leeuwenhoek who discovered blood cells, as well as bacteria, parasites, and many other microscopic creatures. His research finds, which were widely circulated, opened up an entirely new world of microscopic life to scientists.

Leeuwenhoek continued his scientific observations until the last days of his life. After his death, the pastor of the New Church in the Dutch city of Delft, where Leeuwenhoek lived and died, wrote the following:

> *Antonie van Leeuwenhoek considered that what is true in [nature] can be most fruitfully investigated by the experimental method, supported by the evidence of the senses; for which reason, by diligence and tireless labor he made with his own hand certain most excellent lenses, with the aid of which he discovered many secrets of Nature, now famous throughout the . . . World.*

3 Germ Fighting in Modern History

Now that scientists could actually see microscopic creatures, they could begin to do something about fighting dangerous germs. One of the worst diseases of the eighteenth century was smallpox, which spread with frightening speed. What made it even more frightening was that most of those who died were babies and young children. Those who lived were often left disfigured or blind. Lady Mary Wortley Montague wasn't a doctor. She was the wife of a British ambassador to the Turkish court. But she was both a careful observer and a worried mother with a small son. In Istanbul, capital of Turkey, doctors were trying to protect their patients against smallpox through the practice of inoculation. This meant spreading matter from a smallpox scab onto an open wound. This resulted in a mild dose of smallpox that would give the patient immunity to the disease.

Lady Montague had her own son inoculated in Turkey. When she and her family returned to England, she promoted the idea of inoculation. At first everyone was overjoyed at the thought that there might be a cure for smallpox. But then it was discovered that inoculation was not without risk.

Some people became carriers of smallpox, spreading it to others even though they themselves didn't get sick. Other people died from the weak dose of smallpox from the inoculation.

An English doctor, Edward Jenner (1749–1823), who treated the people of Berkeley, a country village in Gloucestershire, found that the local folk, who were mostly farmers working with cows, refused any inoculations. It wasn't because they were afraid but because they claimed to be immune to smallpox. Why was this so? The farmers said that cowpox, a mild but related disease that most of them had already caught, gave them that immunity. In 1788, Gloucestershire was struck by smallpox. Sure enough, Jenner realized that those of his patients who had worked with cows and had gotten cowpox did not get smallpox.

But Jenner now needed firm proof. On May 14, 1796, he inoculated a boy (with the

Lady Montague was scarred by smallpox and lost her younger brother to the disease. After inoculating her own children, she used her social status to encourage vaccinations in England.

father's permission) with cowpox. As expected, the boy did get cowpox. Then, on July 1, 1796, Jenner inoculated the boy with smallpox. Jenner must have been terrified that this wouldn't work. If the boy died, he would be responsible. But the boy did not get ill. Jenner repeated the test twenty-three times and twenty-three times it worked. There could be no doubt: The farm folks were right! Those who had recovered from cowpox were indeed immune. And there were no dangerous side effects or deaths.

In 1796, Jenner tested his cowpox vaccination on a boy named James Phipps. Nowadays, vaccinations are tested in the lab and on animals before being used on human subjects.

Jenner knew that the new treatment needed a new name so that people wouldn't confuse it with the older, dangerous form of inoculation. He called it vaccination, a word meaning "from a cow." In 1798, he published his findings as *An Inquiry into the Causes and Effects of the Variolae Vaccinae, a Disease Known by the Name of Cow Pox*. At first there was a great deal of opposition from other doctors. The

The idea of inoculation was still a new one to people of Jenner's time. This famous 1801 cartoon by James Gillray played on people's fears and confusions about the effects of vaccinations. The scene is the Smallpox Inoculation Hospital at St. Pancras, where the poor were treated.

newspapers took up the issue, making fun of Jenner and publishing a cartoon that showed cows coming out of vaccinated people's bodies. But then members of the British royal family were vaccinated. That broke the resistance. Jenner received two grants, one in 1802 and a second in 1806. He did not live to see the day, but in 1840 vaccination against smallpox was made free for all babies. Vaccination against smallpox became mandatory in 1853.

At the same time that Jenner was doing his work, a German doctor, Friedrich Gustav Jacob Henle (1809–1885), was studying cells and theories of disease. In

1840, he published an article, "On Miasmas and Contagions and on the Miasmatic-Contagious Diseases." In it, he put forth the belief that miasma (vapor in the air) was not the cause of disease. Instead, he blamed carriers of disease that were actual living beings. In his article, Henle wrote, "The material of contagions is not only an organic but a living one and is indeed endowed with a life of its own, which is, in relation to the diseased body, a parasite organism." Unfortunately, though, he was unable to prove that those living things were the actual cause of disease.

One of the saddest stories in the ongoing study of germs is that of Ignaz Philipp Semmelweis (1818–1865), a doctor and obstetrician. In the late 1840s, he was practicing at the Vienna General Hospital in Vienna, Austria, where a horrifying 13 percent of new mothers and their babies died. What gave him the clue was that almost all of them died of the same disease, puerperal fever, also called childbed fever. Semmelweis discovered that puerperal fever was contagious—and that doctors were to blame. They were spreading the disease by not cleaning their hands after performing autopsies. Semmelweis started the practice of doctors washing their hands with a sterile solution before examining women and babies. The death rate promptly dropped to a little higher than 2 percent.

Unfortunately, Semmelweis was abnormally afraid of public speaking or even of expressing himself in writing. As a result, he was often misunderstood or overlooked. Other doctors disapproved of him and said as much. But even though they ridiculed him, Semmelweis refused to back down. In 1861, he published *The Etiology, Concept and Prophylaxis of Childbirth Fever*. But his mind was beginning to weaken under all the attacks of other doctors. Not long after publication of his work, he suffered the onset of mental illness. He died in an insane asylum. His contributions weren't recognized until several years later.

The next person to uncover some of the mysteries of dangerous germs was a French scientist, Louis Pasteur (1822–1895). As a chemist working with the wine industry, Pasteur started his career studying the structure of crystals. But he soon became fascinated with bacteriology, the study of bacteria. Up until that time, scientists still believed in the theory known as spontaneous generation, in which living things, like

Semmelweis's solution to puerperal fever seems simple today. But at the time, the role of germs in infection was still not well understood. Other doctors resisted his methods because they were jealous of his success and doubted his theories.

germs, could spring up from nonliving things, like earth. Pasteur proved that even microscopic creatures could only come from other microscopic creatures.

In the early 1860s, Pasteur made one of his greatest discoveries. He realized that the reason that wine sometimes turned sour was because germs had gotten into the wine, and he found a way to kill those germs through controlled application of heat. Pasteur used his newly discovered method to preserve milk and beer as well. The process came to be named after him and is called pasteurization. Pasteur also solved the mystery of the dying silkworms, which was endangering the French silk industry. It turned out that a germ was attacking silkworm eggs, killing the worms. Pasteur showed the silk industry that by getting rid of the germ, the disease disappeared. He became known as the savior of the silk industry.

This 1885 painting by Albert Edelfelt portrays Pasteur in his laboratory. The son of a tanner, Pasteur was not a particularly good student until he discovered chemistry and science.

Still another of Pasteur's great achievements was his proof that

These laboratory instruments were used by Louis Pasteur. Pasteur was the first to understand the role of germs in health, and his germ theory is one of the foundations of modern medicine.

many diseases are caused by germs that multiply in the body. He also proved what Edward Jenner had only begun to realize. If germs were weakened in a laboratory and then placed in an animal's body, the animal became immune to the germ. Pasteur used his improved method of vaccination to vaccinate sheep against a disease called anthrax. He proved that vaccination could be used against other animal diseases as well.

In 1881, Pasteur made the last of his great discoveries. He had been studying rabies, a very dangerous disease that still infects wild animals and occasionally tame animals and humans as well. In the nineteenth century, rabies was a deadly disease with no known cure. Pasteur came up with an experimental vaccine but had yet to test it. Then, in 1885, frantic parents brought their son to Pasteur. A rabid dog had just bitten the boy, and if he wasn't treated right away he would die. Pasteur warned the parents that his vaccine was experimental, but there wasn't any choice if the boy was to survive. Pasteur used the new vaccine on the boy—and it saved his life. Rabies was no longer incurable.

Another scientist built on the work of Pasteur. This was Joseph Lister (1827–1912), a British surgeon at the Glasgow Royal Infirmary in Scotland. For years, it had been believed that infection was caused solely by bad air. Wound sepsis—the term for a wound overcome by infection—was thought to occur when the injured area started to decompose. But so many patients were dying of what was called, for want of a better term, hospital disease—up to 50 percent of amputation cases, for instance—that Lister suspected there was something more than the air at work. He did his best to encourage the safe healing of wounds, and then tried to find a likely cause for these infections. Could it, he wondered, be the fault of some "pollen-like dust" that got into the wound?

Then, in 1865, Lister heard of Pasteur's work and made the connection between germs in the air and wound sepsis. The germs had to be destroyed before they entered a wound. He knew that carbolic acid had been successfully used to rid cattle of a

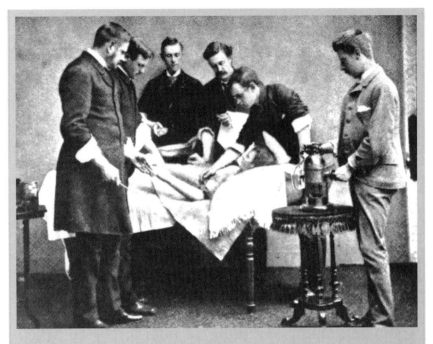

This image shows a nineteenth-century operation using Lister's antiseptic spray. Like Semmelweis, Lister encountered resistance to his methods of preventing infection. By this time, however, the role of germs was better understood, and Lister was a persistent and effective spokesman for his cause.

disease-causing parasite, and he started cleaning wounds with a solution of carbolic acid. In 1867, he announced that his wards at the infirmary had been free from sepsis for nine months. By the 1870s, German surgeons began practicing what came to be called antiseptic surgery. This included the use of sterilized instruments. But in the United States and Lister's native England, doctors weren't so approving. They didn't believe Lister's germ theory and wanted valid proof. On October 26, 1877, Lister carried out an operation under antiseptic conditions and made sure that the success of the operation was both witnessed and well publicized. From then on, antiseptic surgery became accepted almost everywhere. This fact almost completely eliminated postsurgical infections.

A German doctor named Robert Koch (1843–1910) followed the work of Lister. In 1872, Koch investigated anthrax, the disease Pasteur had stopped with his vaccine. Koch studied the blood of infected animals and found the actual disease-causing germ, a type of bacteria. He published two articles, one in 1876 and another the following year, describing his findings and a way to study bacteria and even photograph them. In 1877, he also published a book listing the steps needed to learn what germ causes what disease. Scientists are still using what are now called Koch's postulates:

1) The microbe must be present in every case of the disease, but not present in healthy animals.
2) The microbe must be capable of being isolated and grown in a laboratory culture.
3) After growth in a pure culture, the microbe must be able to reproduce the same disease in a healthy animal.
4) The microbe must be isolated again from the newly infected animal.

Koch's next important discovery came in 1882, when he found the germ that caused tuberculosis.

Discovery followed discovery. In the early 1880s, he found a way to grow bacterial cultures for study in substances such as gelatin. In 1883 and 1884, he found the germ causing a cholera epidemic in Egypt and India. The year 1891 saw Koch founding the Institute for Infectious Disease in Berlin, the first of its kind. In 1897, Koch found the germ causing rinderpest, a cattle-killing disease in South Africa, and came up with the cure. In 1905, he went on to study the mosquito-borne African disease called sleeping sickness. As a result of all his achievements, in 1905 Koch received the Nobel Prize for medicine.

At the same time that Koch was figuring out how to grow bacterial cultures, a Danish scientist was developing a way to classify bacteria by staining them. His name was Hans Christian Gram (1853–1938). In 1884, Gram discovered that bacteria could be divided into two classes, which he called Gram-positive and Gram-negative. Gram-positive bacteria have thick cell walls that stain purple. Gram-positive infections tend to cause high fever. Gram-negative bacteria have thinner cell walls and stain pink. Gram-negative infections tend to cause shock and sometimes death. Gram was a rather shy and modest man. Even though the technique bears his name, he wrote humbly, "I have . . . published the method, although I am aware that as yet it is very defective and imperfect; but it is hoped that also in the hands of other investigations it will turn out to be useful."

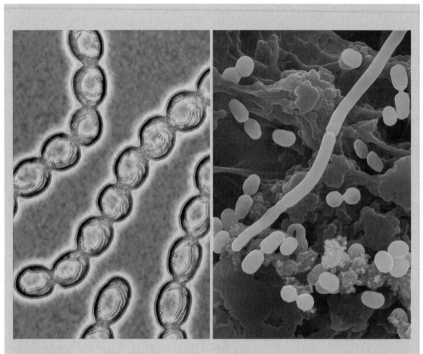

At left, a Gram-positive streptococcus bacteria. They may be carried harmlessly or cause tonsillitis, blood poisoning, and other infections. At right, a Gram-negative streptococcus bacteria. They tend to cause skin and wound infections, in addition to pneumonia.

At the end of the nineteenth century, the age of antibiotics arrived. A French scientist named Paul Vuillemin coined the term "antibiotic" in 1889. In Greek, the word literally means "against life," and it comes from a natural process Vuillemin discovered called antibiosis. This is an association between two organisms, such as germs, that is harmful to one of them. Antibiotics are chemical substances, natural or synthetic (artificially created), that destroy or restrain harmful bacteria.

Sir Alexander Fleming (1881–1955) was a British scientist at St. Mary's Hospital at the University of

London. In 1928, he quite accidentally discovered the germ-killing power of *Penicillium notatum*, the scientific name of a mold from which the life-saving antibiotic, penicillin, was first purified. By chance, he had forgotten about a culture plate he had left with some bacteria on it. When he returned, Fleming was astonished to find that a tiny bit of the *Penicillium* mold had sprouted in the plate and killed all the bacteria around it. The discovery was to open up a new era for medicine—eventually.

Unfortunately, nobody did much with that discovery until 1940. Then two British scientists, Howard Florey and Ernst Chain, found that penicillin protected mice against a number of bacteria, and the development of penicillin for treating humans raced forward. It was just in time to save soldiers' lives during World War II. Fleming, Florey, and Chain shared the 1945 Nobel Prize in medicine for their discovery.

Fleming's accidental discovery was a turning point for medicine. For the first time, doctors had an effective treatment for pneumonia, diphtheria, scarlet fever, and other infections.

Antibiotics such as penicillin *(above)* have saved millions of lives. However, doctors are now concerned that they are being overused, which may lead to antibiotic-resistant bacteria.

By the end of the 1940s, penicillin was available for general use in everyday life.

Following this discovery, other researchers soon began discovering and classifying antibiotics and their effects. There are several types of antibiotics. They include penicillins, cephalosporins, aminoglycosides, chloramphenicol, tetracycline, macrolides, and antifungals. They're all related, but they are different enough in their chemical structure so that each type can attack a different type of dangerous germ.

4 The Future of Germ Fighting

Today we take for granted that we can be protected against many germ-caused diseases. Products that must be germ-free, such as a doctor's scalpel or a dentist's drill, are sterilized. A sterile object has no living germs on it. Proper sterilization is done by heat or radiation—emissions from radioactive material. If you need to remove a splinter at home, you may heat a needle to sterilize it first. Steam is used to sterilize medical instruments. Bacterial spores, the hard, protective coats that bacteria can grow around themselves, can resist even boiling water. But they can be killed by high-pressure steam. Being heated to 113° Fahrenheit (45° Celsius) kills some viruses. Others are so tough that they must be killed by radiation.

We also use disinfectants. A disinfectant is a substance that destroys germs on nonliving things, like clothes or floors. Disinfectants are added to a city's sewage system to keep it from spreading dangerous germs. They are also used in hospitals. At home, though, household disinfectants are usually so mild that plain soap and water are just as useful.

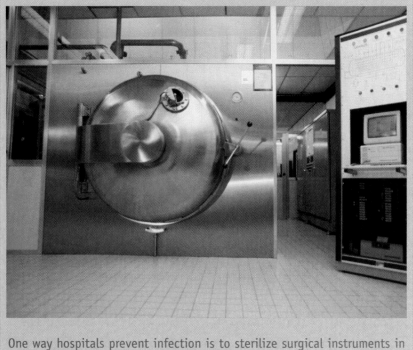

One way hospitals prevent infection is to sterilize surgical instruments in an autoclave like this one. Autoclaves use high heat and steam, or even radiation, to kill bacteria on instrument surfaces.

There are several basic types of disinfectant. These include:

1) Alcohol: This nondrinkable form of alcohol is used, for instance, to disinfect thermometers.
2) Formaldehyde: Used by hospitals to disinfect equipment.
3) Hypochlorites: Including chlorine bleach, these are commonly found in household detergents, as well as in sewage treatment plants.
4) Iodophors: These contain iodine and are used to disinfect large areas in hospitals.

5) Phenols: These are used to disinfect floors, garbage cans, and the like.

Then there are vaccinations to protect us. In the United States, Canada, and other countries, people are vaccinated as very young children against many diseases, such as smallpox, polio, measles, tetanus, and many others. We immunize our pets against rabies. There are four main types of vaccine:

1) Live attenuated vaccines: These contain germs that have been altered so they can't cause disease. Some examples of live attenuated vaccines are measles and chicken pox vaccines.
2) Killed vaccines: These contain killed germs. The various forms of influenza (flu) vaccines are of this type.
3) Toxoid vaccines: These contain toxins (or poisons) from the disease germs that have been made harmless. This type includes diphtheria and tetanus vaccines.
4) Component vaccines: These contain parts of the whole germ. Examples of this type are the hepatitis A and B vaccines.

We will probably continue to see vaccinations as the best way to deal with dangerous germs, at least in the near future. It's the most practical method we now have. One major problem is already at hand with

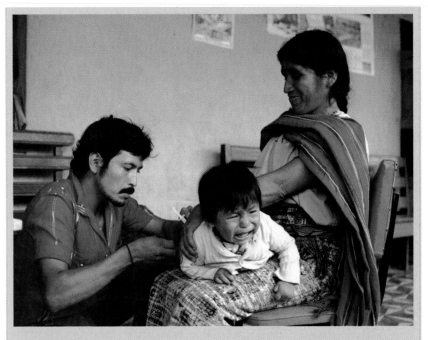

A Guatemalan woman holds her child as the clinic doctor administers a vaccination. Vaccinations for polio, measles, mumps, and smallpox have greatly reduced those diseases worldwide.

antibiotics. Some germs are developing resistance to antibiotics. This can happen through mutation. Mutations are changes that occur in a germ's genetic material, or deoxyribonucleic acid (DNA). This can also happen from the transfer of DNA from one germ to another, creating a new, drug-resistant strain.

But one of the biggest reasons for these changes has to do with the misuse of antibiotics. Not every disease needs to be treated with antibiotics, or can be treated with them. Two main types of germs— bacteria and viruses—cause most infections, but while antibiotics can kill bacteria, they do not work against viruses. And it is viruses that cause colds, the flu, and most sore throats. Just the same, every year, antibiotics are given to treat illnesses that can't be cured by them. This exposure to antibiotics that can't kill them gives viruses a chance to mutate and grow stronger. The same thing happens when a patient is told to take an antibiotic for ten days, yet stops after eight because he or she feels better. Only the weaker bacteria will have been killed. The stronger ones live on. This creates a stronger breed of germ.

Another possible problem may be the use and overuse of antibacterial products such as soaps and detergents. There's no real evidence that using a germ-killing soap at home does any real good. Instead, those products belong in hospitals. Still another problem is the use of antibiotics in our food. Antibiotics are sometimes sprayed onto food plants for disease control. Antibiotics are also used to treat and prevent diseases in

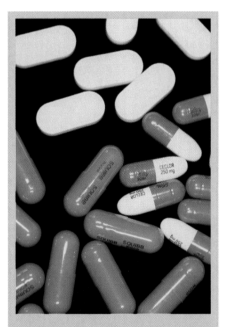

Some common antibiotics have been overprescribed in the last few decades. This increases the likelihood that new treatments will have to be found for antibiotic-resistant diseases in the future.

food-producing animals, as well as to improve their growth rate.

Scientists agree that in the future there must be more careful use of antibiotics, and equally careful studying of any drug-resistant infections. There must also be more research into the ways that germs escape drugs so that new, more effective drugs can be developed.

One possibility for fighting disease-causing germs in the future may be drugs that are designed to match a patient's DNA and specific characteristics. The idea is called personalized medicine. In the future, everyone may carry special genetic-profile information cards. Then, if someone falls ill, the information card will give doctors the data to prescribe a precise and accurate treatment for that person.

What diseases will be cured in the future can't be known. Whether new or mutated germs will cause new problems is uncertain, too. But one thing seems certain. Germs have been around for a long time. In the future, there will still be helpful and dangerous germs. And there will still be scientists who make amazing medical discoveries.

Glossary

antibiotic A substance that can destroy or inhibit the growth of germs.

antibody A substance made in the body that destroys or weakens germs.

bacteria A single-celled organism, some species of which cause disease.

immunize To protect against disease.

inoculation Treatment with a vaccine, a serum made with weakened or dead germs to stimulate the immune system's production of antibodies against those germs.

microorganism A living creature of microscopic size.

pasteurization The process of heating to kill bacteria; the name comes from its discoverer, Louis Pasteur.

penicillin An antibiotic made from a type of mold.

vaccine A preparation containing weakened or dead germs that can no longer cause disease but "trains" the immune system to recognize and kill those germs.

virus A capsule of genetic material that, once inside living cells, replicates itself rapidly and can cause disease.

For More Information

Canadian International Development Agency
200 Promenade du Portage
Hull, PQ K1A 0G4
Canada
(819) 997-5006 or (800) 230-6349
Web site: http://www.acdi-cida.gc.ca

Centers for Disease Control and Prevention
1600 Clifton Road
Atlanta, GA 30333
(404) 637-3534 or (800) 311-3435
Web site: http://www.cdc.gov/3select.htm

National Institutes of Health
9000 Rockville Pike
Bethesda, MD 20892
(301) 496-4000
E-mail: NIHinfo@od.nih.gov
Web site: http://www.nih.gov

The U.S. Department of Health and
    Human Services
200 Independence Avenue SW
Washington, DC 20201
(202) 619-0257 or (877) 696-6775
Web site: http://www.hhs.gov

The World Health Organization
Avenue Appia 20
1211 Geneva 27
Switzerland
(+ 41 22) 791 21 11
Web site: http://www.who.int/en

Web Sites

Due to the changing nature of Internet links,
the Rosen Publishing Group, Inc., has developed
an online list of Web sites related to the subject
of this book. This site is updated regularly.
Please use this link to access the list:

http://www.rosenlinks.com/germ/waag

For Further Reading

Brown, Jack. *Don't Touch That Doorknob! How Germs Can Zap You and How You Can Zap Back*. New York: Warner Books, 2001.

Hyde, Margaret O., and Elizabeth H. Forsyth. *The Disease Book: A Kid's Guide*. New York: Walker & Company, 1997.

Jakab, E. A. M. *Louis Pasteur: Hunting Killer Germs*. New York: McGraw-Hill, 2000.

LeMaster, Leslie Jean. *Bacteria and Viruses*. Chicago: Children's Press, 1985.

Patent, Dorothy Hinshaw. *Germs!* New York: Holiday House, 1983.

Tierno, Philip M., Jr. *The Secret Life of Germs: Observations of a Microbe Hunter*. New York: Anchor, 2002.

Bibliography

Andrewes, Christopher Howard. *The Natural History of Viruses*. London: Weidenfeld & Nicolson, 1967.

Bryan, Arthur H., and Charles G. Bryan. *Bacteriology: Principles and Practice*. New York: Barnes & Noble, 1960.

Buchanan, Estelle Denis, and Robert E. Buchanan. *Bacteriology*. New York: Macmillan, 1951.

Gillies, Robert Reid. *Bacteriology Illustrated*. Baltimore: Williams & Wilkins, 1973.

Knipe, David M., and Peter M. Howley, eds. *Fundamental Virology*. Philadelphia: Lippincott Williams & Wilkins, 2001.

Kurstak, Christine, and Edouard Kurstak. *Human and Related Viruses*. New York: Academic Press, 1977.

Index

About the Author

Josepha Sherman is a professional author and folklorist, with more than 40 books and 125 short stories and articles in print. She is an active member of the Authors Guild and the Science Fiction Writers of America.

Photo Credits

Cover, pp. 6, 9 © Eye of Science/Photo Researchers, Inc.; pp. 1, 3, 4, 11, 15, 20, 35, 41–48 courtesy of Public Health Image Library/Centers for Disease Control and Prevention; p. 5 © NIBSC/Photo Researchers, Inc.; p. 7 © Bettmann/Corbis; p. 12 Pfizer Inc; pp. 14, 18, 23, 25 courtesy of National Library of Medicine; p. 16 Wellcome Library, London; p. 21 History & Special Collections Division/Louise M. Darling Biomedical Library, UCLA; p. 22 © Historical Pictures/Custom Medical Stock Photo; p. 26 © Erich Lessing/Art Resource; p. 27 © Snark/Art Resource; p. 29 © Mary Evans Picture Library/Photo Researchers, Inc.; p. 32 (left) © A. Pasieka/Photo Researchers, Inc.; p. 32 (right) © Dennis Kunkel/PhotoTake; p. 33 © St. Mary's Hospital Medical School/Photo Researchers Inc.; p. 34 © P. Barber/Custom Medical Stock Photo; p. 36 © Collection CNRI/PhotoTake; p. 38 © Bill Gentile/Corbis; p. 39 © Scott Camazine/Photo Researchers, Inc.

Designer: Tom Forget; Editor: Jake Goldberg; Photo Researcher: Sherri Liberman